# A Disbelief of Flesh

Maria-Sophia Christodoulou

Out-Spoken Press
London

Published by Out-Spoken Press,
Unit 39, Containerville
1 Emma Street
London, E2 9FP



A CIP record for this title is available from the British Library.



First edition published 2022
ISBN: 978-1-7399021-3-1

Typeset in Adobe Caslon
Design by Patricia Ferguson
Printed and bound by Print Resources

Out-Spoken Press is supported using public funding by the National Lottery through Arts Council England.

For Yiayia

## Contents

## End

A smokescreen is us breathing into each other's mouths, blue when the sun rises, raising hair from our faces like sad Jesus. In one of our ends, we think of the man who eats opuntia skin. He is tired, like us, fights with his many wives he sees in the water. We realise we are all someone's somebody else, filling ourselves with promises, our voices distant because we choose them to be. God's grey fingers in our eardrums, scrunched with sounds we only hear in the dark. We call on the Holy Mother to forgive the dead for dying.

## Runaway Mother/Land

Twenty-four birds will fly to heaven
so we can feel to feel again.
There is no south, or brain bleed.
In the shapes of every evening
I wait for something to change
your mind Mama. Our dream is sick,
like a dead tooth unremoved, we
are stunted. I have forgotten
what it feels like to make it through
to paradise, pretending all this dying
is make-believe, no longer feeling
our loudness.

## Broken Country

Gut the sun from her eyes
like a soft bomb on soft land.
Mama never had a dream
to be thrown from her home,
now unfed of ghosts. O

she needs an exorcism.

A flare to sleep, she didn't know
this would be the last time
she sat like this, legs
inside legs, hair wrapped
in chicken skin.

## The Last Woman in the Village

Yiayia peels plaster from the walls,
pockets each flake inside her apron.
She is becoming separate people.
To deadhead is to lie with arms
across a table, eyes rolled, the vision
of a church empty of prayer.
There is never a right way to hide—
arranging teaspoons in open spaces,
warding off soldiers like crows.
She grips the village like roots of trees
surrounded by icons of women
in glory, saint men standing—
their hands raised in peace.

## Unfaithful Altars

*—after Athina Papadaki*

I see God blocking the kitchen sink,
adding a teaspoon of sugar
to salad leaves. I see God pouring wine
over the tablecloth, writing
*to be mundane is a sin* in the wine
with his power finger.
I see God demanding the light
be turned on, but I stand
in front of the switch. He tells me
I am going to Hell. I tell him
to wash the plates
in this sinking house.

## Pappou's Hymn

I am a fox carcass
on the side of the road.

Hear the autonomy
between my lungs, miss

and miss the feeling
of return. I sit comforting

my lost in a tomb, mourning
every man and woman lying

beneath my feet.
This is human love:

to be buried with another.
Bodies lie safe under

my watch. I imagine
each corpse nods as I pass.

## Home Cremation

*—Cyprus, 1974*

Mama had never seen a fire spread across a body.
She watched her body, her home, her aunt veiled—
cloth tucked inside her shoe, her cousins cross-legged,
dare to put their fingers in the flames closest.

Mama did not realise how small her body was until
she lived inside sun-dyed tents lined like a saving army,
or a mass grave for the missing without bodies,
for the bodies already buried in forgotten ground.

Mama no longer knew the name of her road or the skin
of her feet embedded within the sand of the Troodos
mountains, her own way of replenishing the taken earth
once blessed by the drinkers of holy water.

Mama could only hear the songs of dying men
sat waiting for their everything to return. A song
she remembers tells the story of a boy who swims
out to sea to find his soul and is never seen again.

## Somewhere in the Hiatus

Saturday mornings were destined
for Yiayia to soothe our cuts
with soaked koulouri, teach us
how to village cook breakfast—
*douse it all in salt and cinnamon.*

Her telling mouth described the status
of every family member.
This is where we named her
a preserver of the unloved.

Now, I am a broken spectator,
the naked behind every picture.
I search for an uncertain end,
while I wait for her
within an antiphon.

## Grief/ing

Have you felt the flesh of it all?
Pushed your hands into soft bread
until you see your prints? My grandmother
was never the type to grind her teeth
or weep from her stomach like bad eggs
on an ugly Sunday in church. In church,
there are so many of her—
clutching her dust-leather handbag,
her shopping tote carrying milk and melons
tucked between each swell of her feet.
Her long skirt filled with coffee-coloured
petticoats. Her blazer pinned with a bead-eyed
insect brooch. Her hair cut short, swept
to the side. Her smile which, for a moment,
makes us wonder if tomorrow
never happened.

## Phantom Pain

I have never heard
the hurt this way,
crushing my handprints
into tomorrow
before tomorrow.
Each day
becomes the sound
of pillows screaming.

It would be kinder
to watch a cadaver
revive itself,
than endure
this leaking ulcer
of bone shudder grief.

## Happy Place

I miss the young-ness
of holiday sea. I miss
morning birds who sing
fainter than sirens.
Danger is everywhere
in this small island. Snakes
become men shooting
from the ground,
Mama tells me:
she hid under red earth
whilst soldiers beat
her orange trees
into pulp,
like the death story
of every goddess
made famous
by a man's word.

Forget praying.
        We have alive
                and no face for miles

## New Home Ritual

In darkness, we bless this house,
burning sage, sighing into our pillows.
I see us lying on stone to cool ourselves,
our children copying, our own colony
of limpets. We search our voices
to suit this newness, planting trees
in the concrete where our children
will split their lips. Talk about before,
lay flowers for memory, breathe
hand-print chairs, open fridges.

Live like this / until the walls / take us in.

## Self-Love Canticle

She impresses me like a hurt.
My skull has throbbed
with her pinkness, smelling
watery like diamond dust.
She keeps her apricots
next to her plants named
after dead lady poets,
believing in sky,
a hot bouquet, a raw kame
waiting for us. Dolour
is how we met in birth,
an angry lake watching
our lives play until the end.
We fear missing it all,
an inflexible light
we cannot step into.

## A Lesson in Moving On

We learn to be safe in this world
in people, not water,
or rock, or the surprise of death.
I am missing the dead
like spasms
of a fortune-telling fish
but if I can, I will be better
in another self, another self and another,
until the world runs out of people
and I am left to fall in love.

## Plum Girl

I empurple my body,
clouds of skin hidden
in a disbelief of flesh.
Every part of me ripens
when accepted. I can't say
the things I should have been—
peace was not an option.
But when the stars had strokes,
their remains fell upon me,
imprinting a feeling of knownness.
I took my eggshell shadow
and morphed into a girl
everyone will remember.

## Acknowledgements

I must start by thanking my Yiayia and Pappou. They taught me love, family, culture; everything that shaped and supported me as I grew up. The grief of losing both of them never gets easier, but I do feel them giving me strength and hope in everything I attempt. My Mum has always encouraged me to read and write, has always been my first supporter. I can only thank her for her patience and forgiveness, showing me my importance and value when I feel it does not exist. Her bravery through every challenge she has experienced is spilled into these poems. Thank you to my Dad who taught me to love history and love my history. So many of these poems are shaped from his lectures about my tiny country. Thank you to my sister Athena for attempting to understand my poems even when, in early drafts, I have no understanding of my poems. Also, thank you for bringing Mariano into the world at a time when we needed someone to love most. Thank you to the people who taught me to write and better my poetry. Firstly, to Jack Underwood, who showed me how to bring life to a poem, as well as exposed me to the brilliant modern poets I am so fortunate to have access to and learn from. To Anthony Anaxagorou, who made my thoughts and feelings about my Cypriot heritage feel noticed on the page. Finally, to the wonderful Wayne Holloway-Smith for believing in these little representations of my life that I call my poems.

## Other titles by Out-Spoken Press

*Cane, Corn & Gully* • Safiya Kamaria Kinshasa

*Apricot* • Katie O'Pray

*Mother of Flip-Flops* • Mukahang Limbu

*Dog Woman* • Helen Quah

*Caviar* • Sarah Fletcher

*Somewhere Something is Burning* • Alice Frecknall

*flinch & air* • Laura Jane Lee

*Fetch Your Mother's Heart* • lisa luxx

*Seder* • Adam Kammerling

*54 Questions for the Man Who Sold a Shotgun to My Father*
Joe Carrick-Varty

*Lasagne* • Wayne Holloway-Smith

*Mutton Rolls* • Arji Manuelpillai

*Contains Mild Peril* • Fran Lock

*Epiphaneia* • Richard Georges

*Stage Invasion: Poetry & the Spoken Word Renaissance*
Pete Bearder

*Nascent* • Vol 1: An Anthology

*Ways of Coping* • Ollie O'Neill

*The Neighbourhood* • Hannah Lowe

*The Games* • Harry Josephine Giles

*Songs My Enemy Taught Me* • Joelle Taylor

*To Sweeten Bitter* • Raymond Antrobus

*Dogtooth* • Fran Lock

*How You Might Know Me* • Sabrina Mahfouz

*Heterogeneous, New & Selected Poems*
Anthony Anaxagorou

*Titanic* • Bridget Minamore

Email: press@outspokenldn.com